Modern Houses of the World

BARRINGTON STUDIO · ILLINOIS · *Harry Weese*
photo: Bill Engdhal, Hedrich-Blessing

Sherban Cantacuzino

MODERN HOUSES
of the world

Studio Vista|Dutton Pictureback
General editor David Herbert

ACKNOWLEDGEMENTS

I would like to thank the following for their valuable suggestions and help in obtaining material: Mr Franco d'Ayala Valva and Mr Julio Faessler in Mexico, Mr Enrique Mindlin and Mr David Plaistow Crease in Brazil, Miss Maria Bottero and Miss Nicky Holland in Italy, Mr John Margetson in Holland, Major and Miss Ek in Finland and Mr Dominic Maillard, Miss Margaret Tallet and Mr Shadrach Woods in France. I am particularly grateful to all the architects, photographers and museums for lending photographs and plans. I am also much indebted to Mr John Donat and Mr Ian McCallum for their advice and to the Hon. Roger Cunliffe for his many suggestions and tireless efforts on my behalf in the United States. My special thanks are due to my secretary, Miss Sasha Wilson, for working under constant pressure.

© Sherban Cantacuzino 1964
Reprinted 1964, 1966, 1970
Designed by Gillian Greenwood
Published in Great Britain by Studio Vista Limited
Blue Star House, Highgate Hill, London, N19
and in the USA by E. P. Dutton and Co Inc
201 Park Avenue South, New York, NY 10003
Set in Plantin 110, 9 pt on 11
Made and printed in Great Britain by
Richard Clay (The Chaucer Press), Ltd, Bungay, Suffolk

UK SBN 289 27970 4

CONTENTS

MARTINS HOUSE · MOZAMBIQUE
A. d'Alpoim Guedes
Photo: Courtesy A. d'Alpoim Guedes

VILLA MAIREA · FINLAND
Alvar Aalto
Photo: Courtesy Museum of
Finnish Architecture

INTRODUCTION

The limited emotional content of architecture makes it the most difficult of all the arts to appreciate. Certain forms, of course, may arouse certain feelings, but it is unlikely that a building will, as a whole, evoke or describe a definite mood—as a poem, a painting or a piece of music or sculpture often do. Nor do the majority of educational systems help to put matters right in teaching literature while they almost totally ignore the visual arts. As a result architecture, the most complex of all visual arts, remains the victim of public indifference.

Architecture is above all a formal art, concerned with such abstract notions as the organization of forms in space and the relationships of the different parts to each other and to the whole. Understanding such a medium is almost entirely an intellectual process. This most people are not prepared to undergo, since the

7

LONG WALL · SUFFOLK · *Philip Dowson*

only feeling aroused is the same sort of pleasure in observing a skill that one has from following the performance of contrapuntal music with a score. An analysis of the technique will only explain the 'how' and not the 'why' of a particular building. It is essential, therefore, to know what we mean by 'emotional content', and to try to understand the language of the architect and the difficulties that are in his way.

The language of architecture includes all those 'literary' associations which lie outside the province of pure form. At one end of the scale there are imitative and descriptive effects, such as the chimneys in the house by Guedes (page 152) or Aalto's clusters of columns and bamboo poles (page 101); and in these instances the quality of description (of cactus plants and tree trunks) is easy enough to appreciate. Niemeyer's flowing shapes (page 146) seem to belong to geology rather than botany, while the evocative quality of Jacqmain's house (page 111) may, more indefinitely, be ascribed to the world of dreams. Architecture, however, has no such ready made vehicle for expressing joy and grief as the major and minor keys of music. At most we might say that pleasure and pride in function can be expressed through such

Photo: Colin Westwood

refinement as the flutings on a Doric column, or the transparency of the roof structure in Saarinen's house (page 44).

Towards the other end of the scale the effects become more and more indefinable, and we resort to stating that curved forms are restful and pointed forms restless, that high spaces express grandeur and low ones cosiness. Movement, dignity, peace, mystery, these are qualities which we all recognize in architecture, and we can even point to certain forms and combinations of forms which contribute towards these qualities. It is what Paul Rudolph means by form expressing the psychology of a building,[1] and its importance has been consistently underrated by architects in their preoccupation with functional problems.

The real difficulties begin when we compare an old building with a modern one. Centuries of construction conceived on the principle of compression, with frequent supports and short spans of beams or arches also mainly in compression, have profoundly affected our subconscious understanding of form. The new materials, steel and reinforced concrete, and the structural techniques which derive from these—cantilevers, large spans, continuous structures, suspension structures or, in other words, the

[1] See also page 62

effect of weightlessness and apparent lack of support—have upset this subconscious appreciation, just as atonal music has upset, in most people, their subconscious understanding of tonality. Yet the new principle of tension and continuity, as Marcel Breuer has pointed out, is so like certain living organisms that we are beginning to show excitement and delight in the new buildings. 'It is the principle of the tree—a structure cantilevered out of the ground, with branches and twigs in turn cantilevered out from the central tree trunk. The reason it stands up is that it is a continuous organism, with all the stresses flowing through all of it continuously.'[1] This is of course an extreme example, not to be found among small buildings like houses, except in the modified form of cantilevers or such suspended elements as sunshades. The Sky house (page 156) is an example of weightlessness, and the Farnsworth house (page 38) an example of the continuous rhythm of a structure where an isolated column or bay has no interest other than technical.

The isolated unit—the doorway, the fireplace, decorated as it used to be—belongs to the conception of enclosed space, of the room with four walls in which holes have first been cut for a utilitarian purpose and then adorned for man's enjoyment. It is a static space, to be appreciated at leisure from one central position. This conception has largely been superseded, with the aid of new materials and techniques, by one where space is in constant flux, and which is unintelligible from one position only, requiring the spectator to move through it in order to appreciate its many-sided and relative qualities. In practical terms the effect of this on architecture was, first, the opening up of the inside of the house and, second, the opening up of the inside to the outside. Every example in this book shows some degree of openness, from the combined living and dining room in the Robie house (page 22) to the open plan embracing all human activities in Rietveld's house (page 75); from the picture view at Rothrist (page 121) to the wide panorama over Lake Garda (page 124); from the

[1] Marcel Breuer, *Sun and Shadow*, Longmans, Green & Co, London; Dodd, Mead & Co, New York

SKY HOUSE · TOKYO · *Kiyonori Kikutake*

deliberate exclusion of the site in the Farnsworth house (page 38) to its deliberate inclusion in the Glass house (page 41).

Perhaps the most fluent expression of this space–time conception was Mies van der Rohe's Barcelona Pavilion (1929), ironically only a temporary exhibition building, but one of the most influential in the history of modern architecture. The old enveloping and uniform character of walls, floors and ceilings has given way to a new freedom where each of these elements has become an independent form. There is no longer any distinction between inside and out, and interior spaces are projected into courtyards by means of walls and overhanging roofs. The walls are just plain slabs and, instead of holes for windows and doors, there are wide openings allowing a continuous flow of space from one part to another.

This opening-up has added a new and rich vocabulary to the architect's language. In the first place it has dictated the need for the control of light and heat from the sun by architectural means. Marcel Breuer has observed[1] that a house on a hill should not have whole walls of glass, because of the glare from the sky, whereas one down in the valley can be more open, as it will be facing the reflected light from the hill-side. Sun-shades, shutters, *brise-soleils* and, particularly, the roof with a deep overhang, are recurrent themes in modern architecture. They are often highly expressive elements, as in the Sky house (page 156) or in the extravagant patterns of *brise-soleils* covering whole façades of glass in the Latin American countries.

Secondly, the expression of spatial continuity through material continuity (a single wall or floor being extended, for instance) has given the plain surface a new eloquence. The walls of the Barcelona Pavilion are faced with marble, and the long seat at the foot of one of these walls, facing the pool, stands distinctly detached. The Noyes house (page 58) has heavy rough stone walls, which form an enclosure on two parallel sides in sharp

[1] Marcel Breuer, *ibid*, page 10

HOUSE AT RHODE-SAINT-GENÈSE · BRUSSELS · *André Jacqmain*
Photo: H. Kessels

contrast to the other two sides of glass. The natural surface is carried through to the inside, and there are no openings whatsoever, except for the gates in the middle. Transparency, so often misunderstood and abused, is here made effective by the contrast with something very solid, while the texture of the stone wall becomes all the more expressive for its independence and continuity.

The argument so far may be restated briefly as follows. There are difficulties in appreciating architecture because of its inherent formal qualities and low emotional content. The complete reversal of structural principles—weight in the air instead of on the ground—has added to our difficulties. But at the same time these new principles, together with the new concept of space, have greatly increased the means of expression in architecture. The master masons of Gothic buildings, within the limitations of the old materials, achieved something very similar, and the proof that the Gothic style has a high emotional content is in its popularity.

Before leaving the general for the more specific subject of this book, however, it is necessary to point to one further difficulty. This is the problem of scale in a contemporary setting. Scale, in an architectural context, is the relationship between man and building, and between one building and another. A smooth plastered wall by itself has no scale, but next to a stone wall it acquires a scale because the unit of a stone has a known relationship to a human being. The scale would become more definite if the wall had a gateway, for here the height and width are truly related to man. We would describe the scale of an ordinary gateway as human, and that of a *porte cochère* as grand. If the scale of one building is sufficiently different from the scale of another close by, we would describe one building as out of scale with the other.

The marvellous quality of a city like Venice is largely due to the infallible instinct for the right scale which its architects and

14

FARNSWORTH HOUSE · ILLINOIS · *Mies van der Rohe*
Photo: Bill Hedrich, Hedrich-Blessing

builders seem to have possessed. It derives from the materials used, and changes only in gradual steps from the brick and stone of the humbler buildings on the small canals to the stone of the churches and palaces in the open space of the Grand Canal and piazzas. There is unity without uniformity, and no sudden change of scale to shatter this unity, as there is, for instance, with the grandiose monument to Victor Emmanuel in Rome. Most cities have suffered from these inflated temples in the last hundred years. Selfridge's is an example in London. It is an expression of misplaced pride in what can be done with traditional forms when wrapping up the new materials.

Such buildings, however, are usually isolated examples and by now, in any case, a thing of the past. More problematic is the change of scale from the regular pattern of window and wall to the emphatic and continuous lines of floor and roof slabs, from the single unit of a stone or brick to the all-glass façade, from the enclosed space of one room to the open space of an entire building. 'We subordinate everything,' says Breuer, 'to the greater unity of this new space. We subordinate the house to the greater unity of the street. We subordinate the streets to the greater unity of the square. We subordinate the squares to the greater unity of the city-space. At the rate at which we move our impressions are quicker, our impressions come in greater units than they ever did before: the scale has changed. . . .'[1] We no longer relate man alone, but man in motion to building. The difficulty, therefore, is not so much in understanding the new scale, as in being able to adjust ourselves from the old scale to the new, especially when the two exist side by side, as in our cities. Obviously, to understand why we receive a shock is going to make that experience less bewildering. The problem, of course, is one for the architects and planners, and in a city like London, with private economic interests taking precedence over planning considerations, incapable of solution.

[1] Marcel Breuer, *ibid*, page 10

'Form expressing the psychology of a building'
TERRACE HOUSES NEAR COPENHAGEN · *Jörn Utzon*
Photo: *K. Helmer-Petersen*

Selfridge's building is, no doubt, an attempt to express dignity. It is the result, not the intention, that we deplore. In modern houses, client and architect have often tried to achieve a dignity worthy of the spiritual side of life. It has been done by using new materials and techniques, and old materials in a new way—like the stone garden walls in Breuer's house (page 51). In other words it has been done by letting the new scale come into play. The accommodation in many of the houses illustrated is often no larger than that of an old cottage, yet the scale is more like that of a modest Georgian country house. Perhaps the most striking example of this is the house at Long Melford (page 69), which is very small indeed, but opened up both inside and to the outside, and spreading eloquently into the landscape.

The modern house can be said to have acted as a receptacle of seemingly infinite capacity for new ideas. Despite the vast and complex building programmes of this age, the house's relative importance probably stood higher in the first half of this century than at any other time in history. The Barcelona Pavilion was not in fact a house, but Mies van der Rohe had made designs for one, based on the same principles, six years earlier. The importance of Wright's early 'prairie' houses (page 22) can hardly be exaggerated, and Le Corbusier's two villas at Garches (page 114) and Poissy remain inescapable points of reference.

TERRACE HOUSES NEAR COPENHAGEN · *Jörn Utzon*
Photo: K. Helmer-Petersen

NOYES HOUSE · CONNECTICUT · *Eliot Noyes*
Photo: *Ezra Stoller*

The impulse of the modern movement springs partly from a social conscience, demanding the correct diagnosis of our ills and the detailed analysis of our requirements. When Gropius founded the Bauhaus in 1919, he set out to reconcile art and industry, thus 'averting mankind's enslavement by the machine, by saving the mass-product and the home from mechanical anarchy and by restoring them to purpose, sense and life'.[1] He taught that collaboration was desirable, to cover the essential technological research on large projects, but that harmonious creation was an ethical problem which could only be solved by the individual. The architect was the co-ordinator controlling every aspect of design, and his aim was to create, with the aid of modern materials and techniques, an environment in which both the basic and the higher forms of living could thrive. Thus we find most of the houses illustrated here conceived as a unity—furnished and decorated, and the gardens laid out, by their architects. Aalto, Jacobsen, Breuer, Mies and Saarinen are also notable furniture designers on a commercial scale, while Jacobsen and Tayler & Green are horticulturists of considerable distinction.

The problem of the house, of designing for family life, has preoccupied nearly every modern architect at one time or another. It is likely to go on doing so, even when good design reaches a well-

[1] Walter Gropius, *Scope of Total Architecture*, Allen & Unwin, London; Harper & Row, New York

GLASS HOUSE · CONNECTICUT · *Philip Johnson*
Photo: Alexandre Georges

organized industry of prefabricated parts. Indeed, the architect's role in prefabrication is paramount if the system is to retain sufficient flexibility to allow for the human factors of individuality and change. The complexity of the problems makes it unlikely that a client will ever be able to choose the component parts from a catalogue and produce a satisfactory whole. After all, in the 19th century and earlier the different functions of a house used to be kept rigidly separate. Now they are often united into a single space. This concentration of activities has led to a new analysis of requirements. The less space we have the more carefully we have to plan it, and often this planning will include the furniture and the garden if any degree of unity is to be achieved. The Schröder house (page 75) is an example of this concentration by the division of daily activities within one space into separate compartments of built-in furniture, while the Sky house (page 156), with its more basic subdivision but less rigid arrangement, is a freer and perhaps more human approach to the same problem.

If an ethical impulse was the principal cause of the revolution in house design, it was certainly not the only one. In the early days of the modern movement few, if any, public institutions or commercial firms were prepared to commission modern architecture. Architects such as Frank Lloyd Wright and Le Corbusier

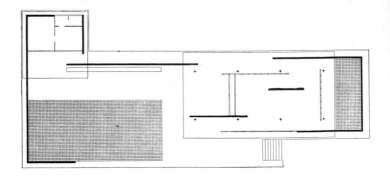

BARCELONA PAVILION · *Mies van der Rohe*

relied largely on a handful of adventurous clients who were prepared to experiment with their own houses. This continued to be
true in the United States between the wars, when Neutra and
Wright led the fight against almost total academic reaction. It
was also true of England in the 1930's, when the few examples of
modern architecture were nearly all houses built by architects
for themselves or for their friends. In England even today the
majority of educated people prefer to play safe and build neo-
Georgian or, understandably in a country full of so many attractive
18th-century houses of modest size, to buy and convert. The
reverse is true of the United States and, since the war, they have
become the leaders, both in quantity and quality, of distinguished
house design. The proportion of American houses in this book,
nearly one-third, reflects this state of affairs and no apology or
further explanation is therefore offered.

An attempt has been made to show the modern house at its
best through the first fifty years or more of its existence. In Frank
Lloyd Wright it reached its early maturity. Holland and Germany
followed suit, with Le Corbusier in France close behind. Italy

20

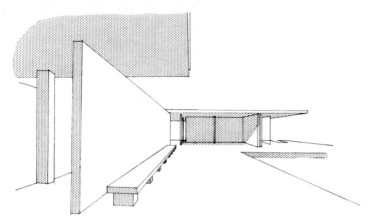

BARCELONA PAVILION · *Mies van der Rohe*

and the Scandinavian countries started late, and Spain and Latin America even later. Differences of climate and geology account for certain fundamental differences in design between one country and another. The degree of industrialization is often in inverse proportion to the compactness of a house, living-in servants being no longer available in the United States and northern Europe. The stage in the industrialization of a country must also affect the standard of execution. To paraphrase the Michelin guide book, the praise conferred on buildings in a region known for its good building should not be compared to that conferred in less favoured parts. On the other hand architects are usually aware of these conditions and will design accordingly, limiting or avoiding industrial techniques and making use of local crafts. Whether the house reflects philosophical attitudes, incorporates artistic theories or demonstrates scientific and technical advances, it is bound to remain a mirror of our civilization at its most sophisticated, just as the country house and the *hôtel particulier* represent to us now the aristocratic way of life and beliefs of a different age.

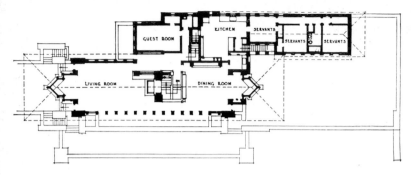

UPPER FLOOR PLAN

Frank Lloyd Wright
ROBIE HOUSE · CHICAGO · USA · 1909

The flat and open landscape of the prairie around Chicago is reflected in the emphatic horizontal lines of the finest of Wright's early 'prairie' houses. Wright had witnessed the economic expansion of the Middle West in its latter stages. With a growing population pushing the frontiers of civilization further and further west, the spirit of the times had been one of adventure and the open road. It is against this dynamic background of continuous movement that Wright's first revolutionary houses must be seen.

The traditional American farm house with its wide openings between reception rooms, and its flexible plan which could be enlarged or reduced as economic or social conditions changed, undoubtedly helped Wright to get his open planning and asymmetrical grouping accepted by his clients.

The open planning in the Robie house occurs at first floor level. It is one great room with a central fireplace, the staircase and

ROBIE HOUSE *Bill Engdahl, Hedrich-Blessing*

dining area on one side and the living area on the other. The unity of the room is emphasized by a continuous window and balcony. More revolutionary still is the way in which the inside is opened up to the outside. The living area juts out into a terrace with a pointed window like an arrow. The terrace, with its enclosing walls and overhanging roof, forms an extension of the room and, with its steps down to the garden, a direct link with the surrounding landscape.

To the powerful imagination shown in these early houses, should be added Wright's technical mastery. Casement windows opening outwards, a central core of utilities, concrete slab foundations laid straight on to the earth incorporating under-floor heating, built-in furniture and lighting, carports instead of garages; these and many other innovations have since become part of the architect's regular grammar of building.

KAUFMAN HOUSE   *Bill Hedrich, Hedrich-Blessing*

Frank Lloyd Wright

KAUFMAN HOUSE · BEAR RUN · PENNSYLVANIA
USA · 1936

Wright admired the Japanese house for its 'supreme study in elimination'. His style was too individual ever to look Japanese. But in the clear articulation of his 'prairie' roofs, in the arrangement of continuous balconies around principal rooms and in his expressive and unadorned use of building materials, he shows his profound understanding of that art.

The Kaufman house is probably Wright's most imaginative work. Here his lifelong preoccupation with elemental statements found complete expression. A large rock was left to form the fireplace and hearth in the living room, for fire was the source of life. From

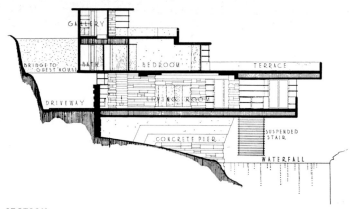

GALLERY

BRIDGE TO
GUEST HOUSE   BATH   BEDROOM   TERRACE

DRIVEWAY   LIVING ROOM

CONCRETE PIER   SUSPENDED
STAIR

WATERFALL

SECTION

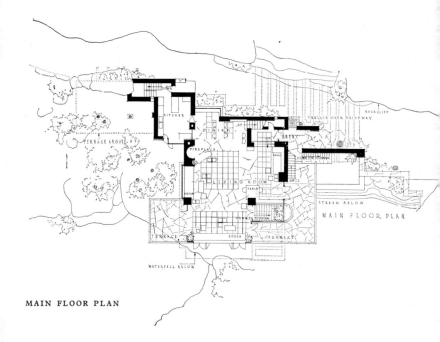

KITCHEN   TRELLIS OVER DRIVEWAY   ROCK CLIFF

TERRACE ABOVE   DINING

TERRACE   ENTRY

LIVING ROOM

STREAM BELOW

MAIN FLOOR PLAN

TERRACE   COUCH   TERRACE

WATERFALL BELOW

MAIN FLOOR PLAN

there you moved through the airy spaces of the rooms and terraces, down to the waterfall and finally on to earth.

The design takes full advantage of the unique site. The living room opens out in many directions on to large terraces and a staircase leads straight down to the waterfall. Bedrooms, too, extend on to terraces and everywhere the structure is projected into the landscape. This was made possible by the use of reinforced concrete, Wright's first consistent use of it in a house. This also enabled him to dispense with the brick mullions of the Robie house and to have, instead, continuous windows emphasizing both the horizontal planes of the terraces and the closeness of indoors and out. This closeness is further emphasized by the use of the same flooring material—stone slabs—inside and out, and by taking the glass of the windows straight into the stone walls without a frame, thus stressing the continuity of the same walling material on both sides of the glass.

Photo Bill Hedrich, Hedrich-Blessing ⇨

KAUFMAN HOUSE   *Bill Hedrich, Hedrich-Blessing*

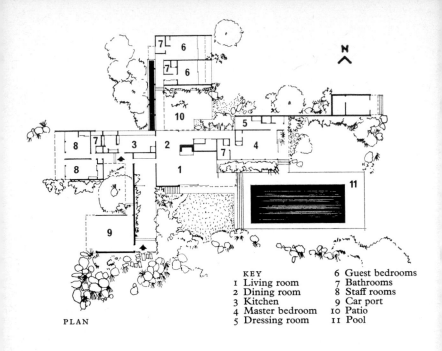

KEY

1 Living room	6 Guest bedrooms
2 Dining room	7 Bathrooms
3 Kitchen	8 Staff rooms
4 Master bedroom	9 Car port
5 Dressing room	10 Patio
	11 Pool

PLAN

Richard J. Neutra

KAUFMANN HOUSE · COLORADO DESERT · USA · 1946

Neutra worked for Wright when he first arrived in America in 1923; and this house, like most of his work, owes something to that master. The close relation of indoors and out is even more developed and the siting of the house, taking full advantage of the magnificent views, reveals an equal sureness of touch. As with Wright's work there is the horizontal emphasis of several roof lines on different planes and the rhythm of continuous windows coming to rest against a solid vertical chimney or parapet wall. But unlike Wright the effect of the forms is restful and urbane. There is nothing elemental in the use of materials. Contrasts in textures are extremely subtle, varying between glass, steel, polished wood, smooth plaster and masonry of a carefully controlled roughness.

KAUFMANN HOUSE   *Julius Shulman*

Two lifelong interests, technology as a means to economy and
the psychology of design, have given Neutra's work its moral force.
The first dates from his years in Berlin after the First World War.
He claims 'typicality as an instrument of perfection' and has never
ceased to search for the typical detail, always simplifying and refin-
ing. The second has given his work a specially human quality.
'The architect must . . . feel responsible for the subtle but vital
preservation and satisfaction of human nerves and of life itself.' A
specific example is the beautiful artificial lighting of the Kaufmann
house, for 'night illumination in a desert oasis has its particular
soul impact and psychological significance after the day glare
reflected from the arid areas'.

KAUFMANN HOUSE   *Julius Shulman*

KAUFMANN HOUSE   *Julius Shulman*

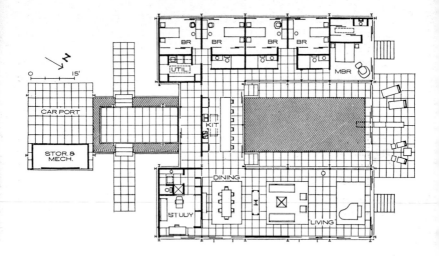

PLAN

Craig Ellwood

DAPHNE HOUSE · HILLSBOROUGH · CALIFORNIA
USA · 1960

Craig Ellwood belongs to the younger generation of architects, and
works in an area which is architecturally one of the most backward,
but industrially perhaps the most advanced, in the United States.
This and his training as an engineer have confirmed him in his
belief that 'industry, science and technology will shape tomorrow's
architecture'. A colleague has remarked that Ellwood is making use
of materials, components and techniques unknown to most architects.[1] This is especially true of the structure and its assembly, and
of the openings between, for which he has developed a wide
repertoire of infilling panels ranging from the fully transparent to
the fully opaque.

The character of this house, that of an open pavilion, may owe
something to the Californian style which developed after 1900 as a
combination of the commercial 'stick' and the more sophisticated

31

[1] Peter Blake, 'Craig Ellwood', *Zodiac 4*, Edizioni di Comunità, Milan

'shingle' styles of the East Coast. The open quality comes from the use of a visible steel structure, infilling panels mainly of glass and the plan itself, which incorporates within the rectilinear structure an open court with a swimming pool. The total absence, uncommon in the Californian climate, of overhanging roofs, is made possible by the use of grey heat-absorbing glass in the windows.

The steel frame, which was erected on site in three days, carries a floor structure which hovers over the ground and looks suspended, but is in fact supported on the ground with the edge cantilevered. Ellwood designed the planting and paving himself, because he wanted his building both firmly related and complementary to the landscape. To this end the recessed floor plays an important part: black pebbles and pools penetrate under the building, giving a continuous effect and throwing the white structure of the building into sharp relief.

DAPHNE HOUSE   *Morley Baer*

DAPHNE HOUSE *Morley Baer*

DAPHNE HOUSE *Morley Baer*

DAPHNE HOUSE   *Morley Baer*

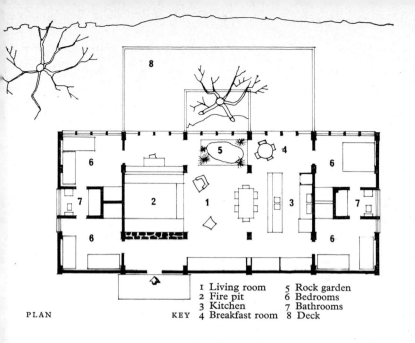

PLAN	KEY

1 Living room   5 Rock garden
2 Fire pit   6 Bedrooms
3 Kitchen   7 Bathrooms
4 Breakfast room   8 Deck

Henrik Bull

KLAUSSEN–BROWN–BALDWIN HOUSE
SQUAW VALLEY · CALIFORNIA · USA · 1959

This house, too, hovers over the ground, but for different reasons. The tradition of the primitive forest shelter, made of local timber and raised above the ground to ventilate the floor, has here been developed exactly to the right degree of sophistication. The site is magnificent: a wood, massive boulders and a steep slope down to a mountain stream. This has been left undisturbed and the point stressed by allowing a tree to penetrate the deck and a boulder the floor of the living room.

Despite its simple rectilinear plan and near symmetry, the house makes a dynamic effect in the landscape comparable, if due allowance is made for the very different scale, to Wright's Kaufman house (page 24). This is because both architects use the structure

35

KLAUSSEN–BROWN–BALDWIN HOUSE   *Henrik Bull*

in an expressive way. Bull uses old timber baulks from railway
snowsheds, blackened with soot from engine smoke, and projects
the beams well beyond the walls of the house. Even more drama-
tically than Wright, he has brought the landscape into the house.
By standing near the boulder in the living room and looking first
at the boulder and then through the cut-out in the deck, one's eye
is projected with an intelligible sense of continuity, deep down into
the mountain stream.

KLAUSSEN–BROWN–BALDWIN HOUSE *Stone and Steccati*

Stone and Steccati

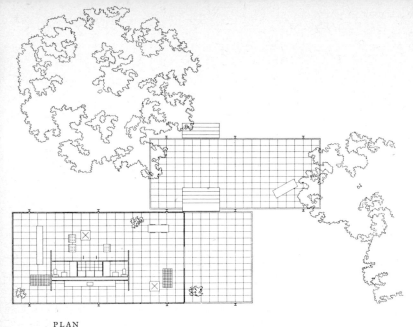

PLAN

L. Mies van der Rohe

FARNSWORTH HOUSE · PLANO · ILLINOIS · USA
1951 (DESIGNED 1946)

Probably the most famous modern house in the world and the embodiment of the architect's dictum 'less is more', it has been the object of both eulogy and vilification. While it has earned Mies the reputation of being a ruthless dictator, his supporters have argued that such economy of means expresses the lack of interference on the part of the architect and allows the user of a building complete freedom. But whatever the moral implications, few will deny that the Farnsworth house is both a fine structure and a successful exercise in subtle formal relationships.

The structure consists of two rows of steel columns holding the steel-framed roof and floor slabs, which are suspended from the columns and cantilevered out at each end. The house consists of a

FARNSWORTH HOUSE   *Bill Hedrich, Hedrich-Blessing*

single large room with a central core of utilities and a fly-screened veranda as an outdoor extension at one end. The entrance is via a terrace at an intermediate level. The floor is raised well above ground level because a neighbouring river generally overflows in springtime.

Formal qualities follow from these utilitarian solutions. The floor and roof structure, passing behind the columns, produces a sense of stress. The cantilevered roof at the ends projects the space within the structure into the landscape. Unlike Ellwood's house (page 31), to which it bears a superficial resemblance, the site has been left undisturbed. There is no garden, and so no physical relation between indoors and out except by way of the terrace.

FARNSWORTH HOUSE
Bill Hedrich,
Hedrich-Blessing

Bill Hedrich, Hedrich-Blessing

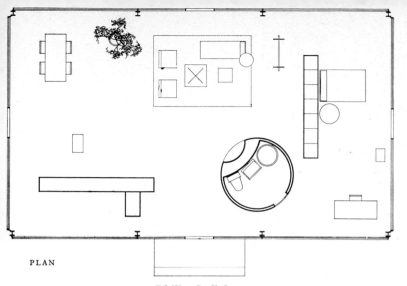

PLAN

Philip C. Johnson
GLASS HOUSE · NEW CANAAN · CONNECTICUT
USA · 1949

The paradox that Mies, the German émigré, built in the Farnsworth house 'a very American house, dynamic, cantilevered, almost in motion', whereas Philip Johnson, the American, built 'a miniature palazzo, static, columnar, serene', has been pointed out by the American architect and critic Peter Blake.[1] Johnson admits his sources to be 1800 and the early modern movement, but his manner is never eclectic.

The Glass house sits on a brick plinth which is only one step above the surrounding lawns. These are in turn surrounded by a low granite rail and by trees which form the real walls. It is the basis of the whole design that the greater volume of the garden belongs to the smaller volume of the house and vice-versa. Standing on one side one can see through to the lawn and trees on the other. The steel frame is painted black—a receding colour—and roof edge and columns are on the same plane. There is no long central core of utilities affecting the transparency of the walls, as in the Farns-

[1] Peter Blake, *The Master Builders*, Gollancz, London; Alfred A. Knopf, New York

GLASS HOUSE   *Alexandre Georges*

worth house. Only the bathroom is enclosed in a solid cylinder, while the low kitchen unit stands separately left of the entrance. All this is quite different to the Farnsworth house which floats above the ground and which has been compared imaginatively to a 'beached yacht' having as its only outdoor areas a 'deck' (the veranda) and a 'dock' (the terrace).[1]

42

[1] Henry-Russell Hitchcock, 'Philip Johnson', *Zodiac 8*, Edizioni di Comunità, Milan

GLASS HOUSE   *Alexandre Georges*

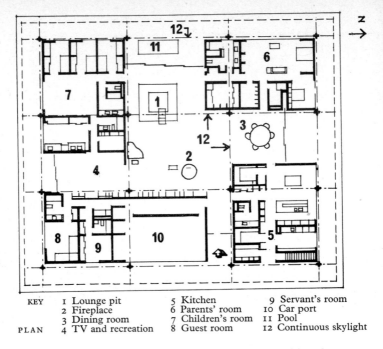

KEY	1 Lounge pit	5 Kitchen	9 Servant's room
	2 Fireplace	6 Parents' room	10 Car port
	3 Dining room	7 Children's room	11 Pool
PLAN	4 TV and recreation	8 Guest room	12 Continuous skylight

Eero Saarinen: Interior by Alexander Girard

IRWIN MILLER HOUSE · COLUMBUS · INDIANA
USA · 1953–1957

One of the only two houses ever designed by Saarinen, this is hardly typical of his work, which includes General Motors Technical Centre, the TWA Terminal Building at Idlewild and the U.S. Embassy in London. His main preoccupation with the synthesis of space and structure and his ability to find widely different and unpredictable solutions are better seen in his larger buildings.

The house is a massive roof, 120 ft × 140 ft, supported on 16 slender columns, the whole sitting on an extended man-made plateau of earth and grass. Under this roof, and on a continuous white terrazzo floor, the four corners are filled in with bedrooms and services, leaving a central space with four large openings con-

44

IRWIN MILLER HOUSE   *Ezra Stoller*

sisting of an entrance with carport and three terraces. Thus the
relation of indoors to out is strictly confined to the structure, while
that of the house to the garden, beautifully laid out on a rectilinear
pattern, recalls the classical manner of the early 18th century.

The cross-shaped columns, standing free of the walls, carry a
welded grid of double steel channels which form bands of skylight.
This opening-up not only lets in additional light where it is needed,
but expresses the structure in a transparent rather than the more
usual solid form.

The sunken sofa pit is the central feature of the lounge. The pit
in Bull's house (page 35) forms an intimate space aside and turns
its back to the dramatic view through the window; in it you face a
solid wall with a fire hearth. Saarinen's pit is out in the open, the
fireplace is elsewhere, and you continue to enjoy the space around
and the view through the window, albeit from a lower angle.

IRWIN MILLER HOUSE   *Ezra Stoller*

IRWIN MILLER HOUSE   *Ezra Stoller*

Robert Damora

Gropius and Breuer

GROPIUS HOUSE · LINCOLN · MASSACHUSETTS · USA
1938

Gropius has defined technology as 'the separation of the essential and super-personal from the personal and accidental'. He has spent a lifetime coming to terms—his own terms—with the machine and believes that the architect's most important task, the solution of socially urgent problems, is an ethical matter requiring a highly developed social conscience. Besides his profound influence as a teacher on a younger generation of architects,[1] Gropius also made a considerable impact on a country just waking up from a long reactionary period with the houses he and Breuer built after their arrival in the United States in 1937.

Gropius' own house is both evidence of his undoctrinaire approach and of his deep concern for the function of a building. The materials used are the traditional weatherboarding of the 'shingle' style, and bare columns and walls are allowed to have their outlines softened by climbing plants. Partial glazing and fly-screening make the porch into an adaptable space for all seasons, from outdoor living in summer to ping-pong in winter.

47

[1] Among them Rudolph and Noyes who are represented on pages 62 and 58 respectively

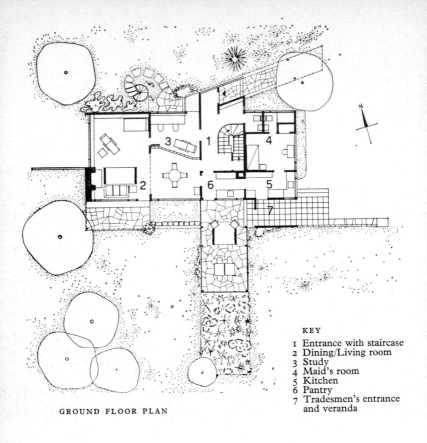

KEY
1 Entrance with staircase
2 Dining/Living room
3 Study
4 Maid's room
5 Kitchen
6 Pantry
7 Tradesmen's entrance
and veranda

GROUND FLOOR PLAN

In a formal sense the house is a cube with some parts pushed out and others cut open. The handling of space is entirely contemporary as in Le Corbusier's house at Garches (page 114) but, unlike that house, realized in traditional materials. This carving up has its beginnings in practical requirements, but Gropius has also created a masterly three-dimensional composition reminding one that the origins of the modern movement lay as much in the formal preoccupations of the cubist and abstract painters as in functionalist doctrines.

48

GROPIUS HOUSE   *Courtesy Professor Gropius*

GROPIUS HOUSE   *Robert Damora*

GROPIUS HOUSE   *Courtesy Professor Gropius*

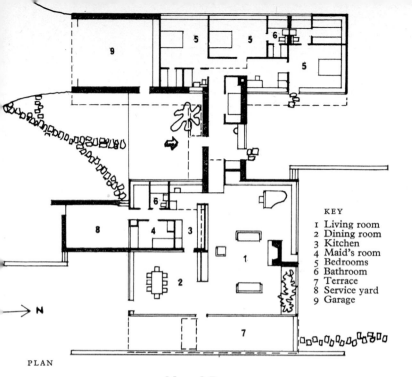

KEY
1 Living room
2 Dining room
3 Kitchen
4 Maid's room
5 Bedrooms
6 Bathroom
7 Terrace
8 Service yard
9 Garage

→ N

PLAN

Marcel Breuer

ROBINSON HOUSE · WILLIAMSTOWN · MASSACHUSETTS USA · 1946–1947

Like Neutra, Breuer is something of a specialist in houses. First a pupil, then a teacher at the Bauhaus, he continued his association with Gropius in the United States until 1941. His exhibition house for the Museum of Modern Art in 1949, which was visited by a large section of the American public, became a supremely succesful advertisement for split-level planning.

The Robinson house is one of Breuer's favourites. 'Often a house with an ample budget tends to become over-complicated with the client's requirements. This was not the case here. The building programme was kept simple and the concept generous.'[1] It is in-

[1] Marcel Breuer, *ibid*, page 10

ROBINSON HOUSE   *Robert Damora*

deed ample generosity and economy of means that form the main characteristics of Breuer's individual style. The restrained and consistent use of wood and stone, and the simple but eloquent roof shapes and sun-shades, come most readily to mind. In this house the 'butterfly' roof follows the shape of a strongly articulated plan dividing day activities from night. The big overhang keeps the midday sun off the living-room windows and protects the terrace, while the cut-out in the overhang lightens the effect from inside the room.

Another characteristic formal device is the low spreading stone walls extending the apparent size of the house and projecting the spectator's view from the house into the landscape of the Berkshire hills. Formal qualities are further emphasized by the use of colours —blue, yellow, grey and white—to differentiate between the planes of garage, entrance, yard and living-room walls.

ROBINSON HOUSE   *Robert Damora*

ROBINSON HOUSE   *Robert Damora*

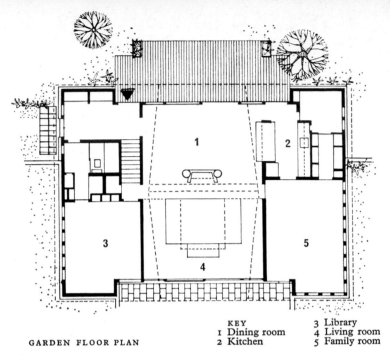

Harry Weese

BARRINGTON STUDIO · BARRINGTON · ILLINOIS
USA · 1958

There is something un-American about this house. The architect's education included a course at the Cranbrook Art Academy
under the Finnish Saarinens. But other reasons may be a reaction
against the years he worked with Skidmore, Owings and Merrill,
the influence of independent spirits like Le Corbusier and Breuer,
or simply that Chicago tends to breed a race of individualists.

The Scandinavian look—shingled pitched roofs and gables, sloping ceilings, boarded walls and round-headed doorways—is in fact
rather superficial. Weese's approach is really formal and humanist.
The plan of the house as well as the garden layout are to all intents
and purposes symmetrical, giving an appearance of quiet dignity.

54

BARRINGTON STUDIO   *Bill Engdahl, Hedrich-Blessing*

The great central living room, which both rises through two storeys and is partly sunk as a sofa pit, forms the hub of all family activities. The suspended bridge, which connects the otherwise unconnected bedroom wings, stresses the centralized and almost Palladian character of the plan.

The house was designed for the architect's family and an informal way of life. The functional aspect was carefully considered, as for instance in the choice of finishes which require little maintenance, in the bedroom balconies and cat ladders which provide direct access to the swimming pool and other outdoor activities, and in the dimmer panel which controls the intensity of the lighting both inside and outside the living room.

BARRINGTON STUDIO ▷
Photo: Bill Engdahl, Hedrich-Blessing

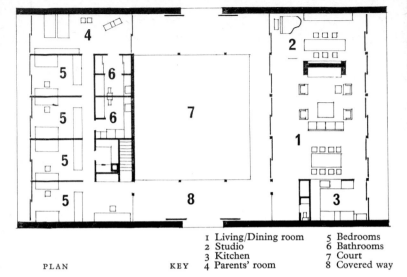

		KEY			
PLAN		1	Living/Dining room	5	Bedrooms
		2	Studio	6	Bathrooms
		3	Kitchen	7	Court
		4	Parents' room	8	Covered way

Eliot Noyes

NOYES HOUSE · NEW CANAAN · CONNECTICUT
USA · 1954

The rugged character of the site has clearly influenced the design of this house, just as the restricted and man-made character of the suburban plot at Hillsborough has influenced Ellwood's design (page 31). But the differences go deeper, despite the similarity in plan and programme. Noyes, who grew up in New England and trained under Gropius and Breuer at Harvard, believes that climatic and geological differences are still a good reason for stressing regional characteristics in building.

The predominant idea of this house, which the architect designed for his own family of four children, dogs, cats and other pets, was to provide, in his own words, 'visual clarity . . . strongly enough to dominate the family activities with their attendant clutter and paraphernalia, and so give a kind of order to all the kinds of living that go on here'.[1] These activities include music, painting,

[1] *Life*, New York, February 15th, 1963

NOYES HOUSE   *Ezra Stoller*

sculpture, photography, business meetings and entertaining. The solution is in the plan and in the choice of materials which clarify the plan. A courtyard and covered link divides day and night activities, and this division is emphasised by the bedroom wing turning its back on the courtyard and facing outwards on to the wood. The courtyard, living-room wing and wood are one continuous space; so when one stands in the living room, the real walls are the solid bathroom block on one side and the trees on the other. The extreme contrast of massive stone walls and glass both clarifies the division and unifies the design, the continuity of the two parallel walls being maintained by glazing at the two ends of the bathroom block. Noyes has described the particular spatial quality of the house as 'intensified by open and shut, wall and window, stone and glass, ceiling and sky . . .'.[1]

[1] *Ibid*

NOYES HOUSE   *Ezra Stoller*

NOYES HOUSE   *Ezra Stoller*

NOYES HOUSE

Ezra Stoller

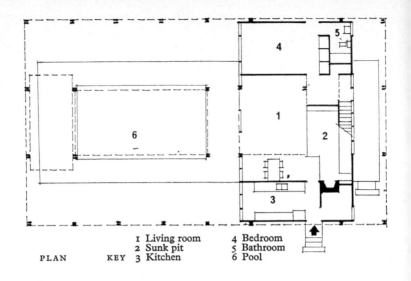

PLAN KEY	1 Living room 4 Bedroom
	2 Sunk pit 5 Bathroom
	3 Kitchen 6 Pool

Paul Rudolph

HISS HOUSE · LIDO KEY · FLORIDA · USA · 1954

Rudolph combines a rigorous technological and structural discipline with an understanding of form which is rare among architects today. He regards functional solutions on their own as totally inadequate and has indicated five other 'determinants of architectural form',[1] the environment created by other buildings, the influence of region, climate and landscape, the choice of materials, the psychological demands of the building and the spirit of the times. It is the last two that are the most difficult to define. 'We must learn how to create a place of worship and inspiration; how to make quiet, enclosed, isolated spaces; spaces full of hustling bustling activities pungent with vitality; dignified, vast, sumptuous, even awe-inspiring spaces, mysterious spaces. . . .'[2] And of the last 'determinant' he says that we should not be ashamed, like the

[1] Paul Rudolph, 'The Six Determinants of Architectural Form', *Architectural Record*, New York, October, 1956   [2] *Ibid*

HISS HOUSE

Renaissance, of using forms because we like them irrespective of their functional purpose and origin.

Two characteristic themes of Rudolph's, which recur in several of his buildings, are groups of small plywood or concrete vaults and, as in this house, the 'umbrella' roof which protects the real roof. Besides giving shade to the open parts of the house, it also lets the breezes pass between the two roofs. His technological bent can be seen in the elegant steel structure of twin columns made rigid at the open end with diagonal tie rods and in the suspended canopy at one end of the pool. The contrast of enclosure and openness, which gives this house much of its character, is stressed by the separation of the structure as belonging to the outside, from the panels and windows which enclose the box-like interior. The simple conception is continued inside with a central double-storey living room and gallery at each end of which there is a bedroom with its own bathroom.

63

HISS HOUSE   *Lionel Freedman*

HISS HOUSE ⇨
Wm. Amick

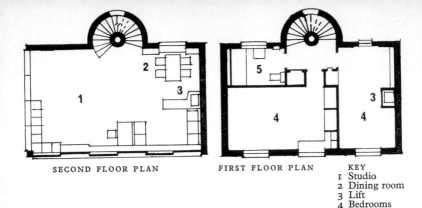

SECOND FLOOR PLAN   FIRST FLOOR PLAN

Tayler and Green

STUDIO HOUSE · HIGHGATE · LONDON · ENGLAND
1940

'A house, largely glass, rising like an Aphrodite from the foam, above the old roofs of surrounding cottages.' Even if the 'largely glass' of Professor Reilly's original description seems a little exaggerated now, the anthropological comparison remains apt. For Tayler and Green, fitness of purpose has always been a guiding principle. 'Instead of super-imposing our own abstract architectural character, we could accentuate the slowly formed and therefore functional character of the business or trade for which we design.'[1] In this case the 'business or trade' was life itself—an artist's life in urban surroundings.

Site restrictions determined a vertical urban solution and the house was planned on three main floors, a basement for storage and a roof garden with part of it as a glazed sitting room. Putting the living rooms on the top floors is a variation on the traditional form of town living, but the vertically open plan with the circular staircase opening out of the rooms shows an entirely contemporary way of handling space. When one climbs the staircase, there is a calculated and effective progression from the relatively small and dark spaces of the lower floors, through the light and airy studio framing restful distant views of London, to the unlimited space of the roof garden and the open sky.

66

[1] Herbert Tayler, 'Shops', *Architectural Review*, London, February, 1957

STUDIO HOUSE
Cracknell

Philip Dowson. Associate: Peter Foggo
LONG WALL · LONG MELFORD · SUFFOLK
ENGLAND · 1963

Philip Dowson and his architects' group within the engineering firm of Ove Arup and Partners, are quietly making a remarkable contribution to architecture in a country where the formal values of a three-dimensional art have consistently been neglected in favour of literary qualities. Though most of their work consists of major industrial and university buildings, this small house is of considerable importance and one of the few built in England since the war which stands comparison with the best foreign examples.

Fine building starts with a predominant idea and ends as a synthesis of form and function. Here the idea was long white screen walls and two dominating horizontal planes—timber roof and brick podium—the garden becoming an extension of the living area under the roof. On the one hand the screen walls divide the carport and service area from the living area, on the other they extend and tie a very small house into the landscape. The podium both raises the living area to take advantage of the view over a gently sloping valley of cornfields and establishes a sense of order on top, symbolizing man's ascendancy over nature. The openness on three sides of the building makes for spatial continuity between inside and out, especially where the external areas of terrace and lawn are contained by the screen walls. The low brick walls, which carry the timber structure, give one a sense of enclosure, especially when sitting down, while the roof overhang and screen walls outside help to give one a sense of identity with the building itself.

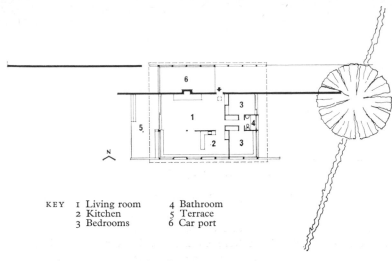

KEY   1 Living room   4 Bathroom
        2 Kitchen   5 Terrace
        3 Bedrooms   6 Car port

PLAN

LONG WALL   *Colin Westwood*

LONG WALL   *Colin Westwood*

LONG WALL   *Philip Dowson*

Serge Chermayeff

CHERMAYEFF HOUSE · HALLAND · SUSSEX
ENGLAND · 1938

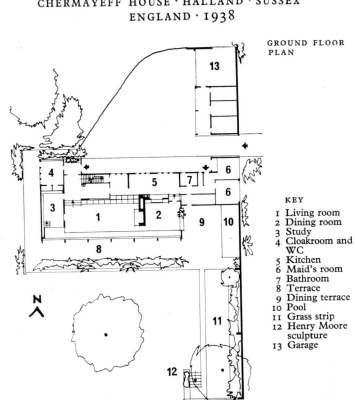

GROUND FLOOR
PLAN

KEY

1 Living room
2 Dining room
3 Study
4 Cloakroom and
  WC
5 Kitchen
6 Maid's room
7 Bathroom
8 Terrace
9 Dining terrace
10 Pool
11 Grass strip
12 Henry Moore
  sculpture
13 Garage

CHERMAYEFF HOUSE   *Courtesy Architectural Review*

Hitler's persecution of artists and intellectuals, combined with England's traditional role of offering asylum, contributed inestimably to English architecture. Though most of the architects who came from Germany had gone to the United States by 1939, the handful of distinguished buildings they designed were enough to give a new impetus to English architects, especially those who, like Maxwell Fry and F. R. S. Yorke, associated with them. Chermayeff's house belongs to this brief but exciting period.

Like the house at Long Melford (page 69), this too has a screen wall and sits on a brick podium. But the main block is set at right angles to the wall and opens up in one direction only, towards the south. The dining room, sitting room and study open out into one another, and this is expressed by the continuous window treatment; while on the first floor a continuous balcony to the bedrooms provides an equivalent openness and consistency. It is from these rooms, especially on the ground floor, that the importance of the screen wall becomes manifest. This importance is stressed by the continuation of the podium or terrace for its full length and by its eloquent ending, in the shape of a trellis, a Henry Moore sculpture and steps down to the lawn. Both the lawn with its tree and the incidents along the wall—dining terrace, pool, grass strip, tree, sculpture, steps and trellis—belong to the interior. Wall and trellis act as a foil: in one direction the view is contained, in another it is open and infinite.

CHERMAYEFF HOUSE   *Courtesy Architectural Review*

CHERMAYEFF HOUSE   *Courtesy Architectural Review*

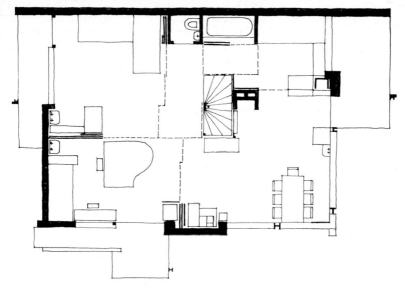

G. Rietveld

SCHRÖDER HOUSE · UTRECHT · HOLLAND · 1924

Historical processes, like biological ones, seem to create, alongside their main evolutionary stream, offshoots which, however remarkable in themselves, are not regenerative. Such an offshoot from the modern movement was the Dutch 'De Stijl' group, with which Rietveld was only loosely associated, but whose formalist tendencies he fully developed in this house.

Building regulations demanded a conventional plan on the ground floor while the first was simply named 'Loft' and subsequently laid out as an open living area subdivided, in the Japanese manner, by sliding screens. The outside seemed to bother the building authorities less, though the ordinary citizen of Utrecht was unable to accept the contrast for several decades.

75

Rietveld conceived the house as a volume defined by planes slotted together like playing cards. The result was an apparent independence of parts and a close relation between inside and out. The methods were overlapping, separation, the use of the same finishes inside and out, and of colour to emphasise recession and projection. Rietveld was more interested in formal qualities than function. For instance no attempt is made at a consistent expression

SCHRÖDER HOUSE   *Jan Versnel*

of the plan through the elevations, and the construction, which looks like continuous concrete slabs, turns out to be plastered brick and wood, except for the balconies which are concrete and steel. His aim, in his own words, was to use 'elementary forms, simple spaces and primary colours exclusively, because they are so fundamental and because they are free of associations',[1] and to do this with the materials and techniques most readily available.

[1] Rietveld, 1924, *Schröder Huis—Quadrat-Print*, de Jong & Co., Hilversum, 1963

SCHRÖDER HOUSE   *Jan Versnel*

J. A. Vryhof

Van den Broek and Bakema

VAN DEN BROEK HOUSE · NEAR ROTTERDAM
HOLLAND · 1954

The effect of 'separation', which Rietveld carried through with such consistency in the Schröder house (page 75), has since become a favourite device with architects for expressing the lightness characteristic of modern materials, for distinguishing between structural and non-structural units, and for articulating structure itself as in certain types of precast concrete design. It can be seen here in the low cupboard along the edge of the sleeping balcony and in the brick wall screening the garden side of the garage.

The particular drama of this house, which stands isolated on the edge of a small canal, is in the contrast of its solid enclosed appearance on the entrance side, with the open garden side. The solidity is emphasised by long window slits in the living room, framing close-up views of grass and bark. The contrast is heightened by the progress from the single storey entrance to the double storey living room with its huge windows looking out high into the trees and sky. Here the conception is very simple, but on the grand scale of a palace. To understand this, it is necessary to study the section as well as the plan. A sleeping balcony cuts into the double storey living room and, with its bold projection outwards and steps down, forms a direct link with the garden. All of this, including the garden, becomes one enormous and continuous space which can only be fully appreciated by moving about in it.

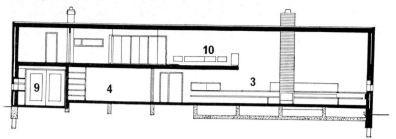

SECTION

KEY

1 Entrance
2 Hall
3 Living room
4 Study
5 Kitchen

6 Cloakroom
7 Parlour
8 Terrace
9 Garage
10 Sleeping balcony on first floor

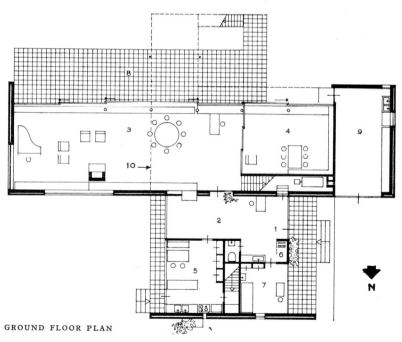

GROUND FLOOR PLAN

N

79

VAN DEN BROEK HOUSE · *Spies*

VAN DEN BROEK HOUSE · · · *Photo: J. A. Vryhof* ⇨

VAN DEN BROEK HOUSE · *J. A. Vryhof*

Arne Jacobsen

TERRACE HOUSES AT KLAMPENBORG
COPENHAGEN · DENMARK · 1950

Two qualities which give Danish domestic architecture a consistently high standard are craftsmanship and fine siting. Craftsmanship is a tradition and is evident everywhere, especially in bricklaying, paintwork and joinery. Fine siting implies both a deep understanding of the lie of the land and careful planting and paving.

Arne Jacobsen, who designed these houses and lives in the one illustrated, runs a considerable practice which includes large industrial schemes, office blocks and schools as well as furniture and textile design. To the native and truly original quality of his work, should be added his inclination towards the abstract and more doctrinaire approach to design evident in the early (1934) white-stucco Bellavista flats next door and, more recently, in his use of the curtain wall.[1] A real feeling for the purity of form is apparent even in the vernacular brick-and-tile idiom of these houses, as for instance in the garden elevation and in the very simple metal balustrade at the top of the staircase.

The staggered arrangement on plan gives privacy and, together with the sloping roofs and chimneys, provides a satisfying rhythm and silhouette. Privacy is also achieved by facing the dining room on to an enclosed courtyard, and by putting the living room up on the first floor with a balcony and an open view towards the sea.

[1] S.A.S. Terminal, Rodovre Town Hall and Jespersen office block

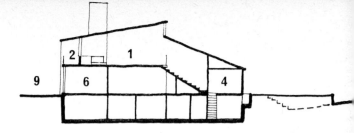

SECTION

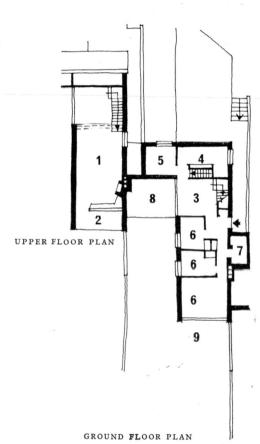

UPPER FLOOR PLAN

KEY

1 Living room
2 Balcony
3 Dining room
4 Kitchen
5 Maid's room
6 Bedrooms
7 Bathrooms
8 Courtyard
9 Garden

GROUND FLOOR PLAN

83

TERRACE HOUSES AT KLAMPENBORG   *Strüwing*

84

HOUSE AT KLAMPENBORG   *Else Tholstrup*

Erik Chr. Sörensen

HOUSE AT KLAMPENBORG · COPENHAGEN DENMARK · 1957

In this house, too, there is plenty of craftsmanship—as, for example, in the kitchen joinery and in the way the turned down edge of the copper roof has been made to look like the top of a delicate cornice. But more striking is the consistent use of a structural system which could be described as a series of broad, U-shaped, reinforced concrete frames lapping up the sides and underneath the building and sitting either on E-shaped frames turned upside down, or on solid walls running at right angles. This is made clear by one part of the structure projecting beyond another at points of support and intersection.

The house, which has been built in the mature grounds of a

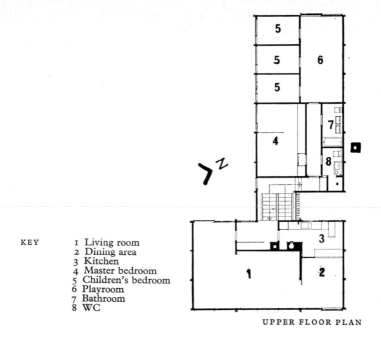

KEY

1 Living room
2 Dining area
3 Kitchen
4 Master bedroom
5 Children's bedroom
6 Playroom
7 Bathroom
8 WC

UPPER FLOOR PLAN

19th-century villa, consists of two pure cubes of glass and white panels, superimposed on an irregular site which retains the contours of an old fortification. One cube, at the lower level, contains bedrooms and children's rooms and sits over a solid basement of services and storage. The higher cube, forming the living area and sitting on stilts over the entrance, is high enough to catch views of the sea. These levels and the corresponding ground levels are linked by three short flights of steps. Thus, even if the forms themselves seem doctrinaire—the free-standing chimney should also be noted in this context—the relationships of the forms reflect the contours of the site.

HOUSE AT KLAMPENBORG

HOUSE AT KLAMPENBORG   *Else Tholstrup*

Else Tholstrup

HOUSE AT KLAMPENBORG   *Else Tholstrup*

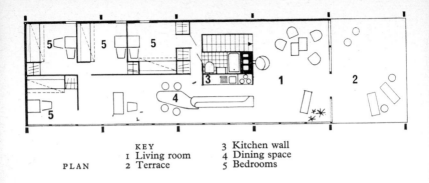

KEY	3 Kitchen wall
1 Living room	4 Dining space
PLAN 2 Terrace	5 Bedrooms

Jörn Utzon

HOUSE NEAR LAKE FÜRESÖ · COPENHAGEN
DENMARK · 1952–1953

One of the recurring themes in modern architecture is the expressiveness of structure. This does not mean merely the expression of structure, but also a demonstrable excitement on the part of the architect in so expressing it. The quiet simplicity of this house may seem far removed from the fantastic shapes of the Sydney Opera House, Utzon's latest work, yet the structure, especially in the overlapping edge beams, is full of movement and has a dynamic spirit comparable to the Farnsworth house (page 38). There is a double row of reinforced concrete columns on the ground floor, the inner row supporting the first floor and the outer columns continuing the full height and supporting the roof.

But the comparison to the American house must not be taken any further. Utzon's house is built on dry land, and this is made clear not only by the solid form of the utility core rising from the ground, but by the unambiguous presence of a canal, and by the valid uses to which the lower floor is put: carport, entrance and covered space with open fireplace for ping-pong, woodcutting and other out-door activities. The house, which leaves the beautiful site undisturbed, is really a pavilion in the trees, turning its back, with bedrooms, on to a road and overlooking a lake on the side of the living room and balcony.

HOUSE NEAR
LAKE FURESÖ

HOUSE NEAR LAKE FURESÖ

K. Helmer-Petersen

HOUSE NEAR LAKE FURESÖ   *K. Helmer-Petersen*

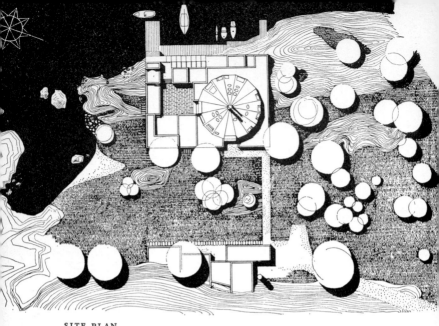

SITE PLAN

Ralph Erskine

HOUSE ON THE ISLAND OF LISÖ
SWEDEN · 1955–1956

In contrast to Utzon's house (page 90), here the site has been man-made and imposed clear-cut and rectilinear by the edge of the sea, upon a wild landscape of rock and forest. An English architect living in Sweden, Erskine is continually searching for a Scandinavian style. The conception of this house envisages three separate areas relating to the three seasons of the Swedish climate; the hemisphere for protection and cosiness in winter, the open but sheltered terraces of the concrete podium in autumn and spring, and the sea and forest in summer. Besides obvious formal attractions, two practical considerations determined the hemispherical shape. It was the most economical space to heat, and the client, who was a director of a light engineering firm, was keen to pre-

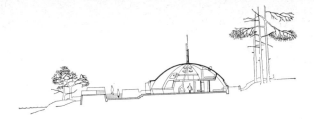

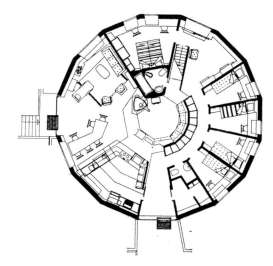

fabricate the sixteen segments of sheet steel himself.

With the exception of the two entrances, all the windows and plastic bubbles follow the spherical shape and have been placed according to need. The shape of a hemisphere rising out of a podium is powerful enough to dominate haphazard patterns. Internally, the arrangement of the living area, openly and freely planned both in the horizontal and vertical direction, is the result of detailed research into the client's requirements. At ground floor level there are areas for cooking and eating, sewing and playing, sitting by day and, perhaps symbolically, around the centre point of the circle, sitting by an open fireplace and television set. A staircase leads to a gallery with a working area and two guest bedrooms.

HOUSE ON LISÖ   *Ralph Erskine*

HOUSE ON LISÖ   *Ralph Erskine*

HOUSE ON LISÖ   *Ralph Erskine*

HOUSE ON LISÖ   *Ralph Erskine*

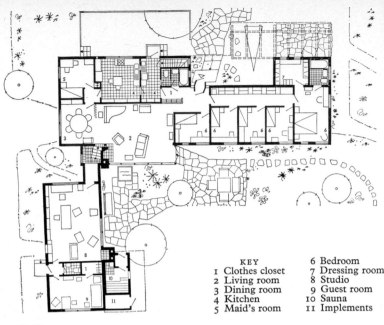

KEY

1	Clothes closet	6 Bedroom
2	Living room	7 Dressing room
3	Dining room	8 Studio
4	Kitchen	9 Guest room
5	Maid's room	10 Sauna
		11 Implements

PLAN

Sven Markelius

MARKELIUS HOUSE · KEVINGE · STOCKHOLM
SWEDEN · 1945

Since the beginning of the century Stockholm (and later other cities) has been carrying out a progressive policy of extensive land acquisition, establishing what Professor Markelius, who now directs this policy as the city's chief planner, has described as 'the principle . . . that a community has a right to decide when and where urban development is to take place'.[1] One effect of this policy has been to build blocks of flats rather than single houses. The considerable cost of building private houses has also made these a comparative rarity and has encouraged a number of Swedish designers to develop prefabricated sections like the wooden units of which this house is constructed.

If Erskine's house (page 94) is consciously striving after a

[1] G. E. Kidder Smith, *Sweden Builds*, Bonniers, Stockholm, 1950

MARKELIUS HOUSE   *Courtesy Professor Markelius*

Swedish style, Markelius's is the more typical. The influence of
the site is paramount: the wilderness of an island and man's predominance over nature—the humanist approach—on the one hand,
the unspoilt suburban plot and the complete integration with the
landscape—the romantic approach—on the other. Both houses
claim to spring from functional requirements. Erskine's does so in a
general sense, accepting the subordination of the individual to
family life as a whole, both in fact (the predominance of the open
plan) and in form (the dome). Markelius's is more specifically
functional in the predominance of the individual room (bed-sitting
rooms for each member of a large family), expressed through an
informal L-shaped plan with traditional pitched roofs and gables.

MARKELIUS HOUSE   *Olof Ekberg*

MARKELIUS HOUSE   *Olof Ekberg*

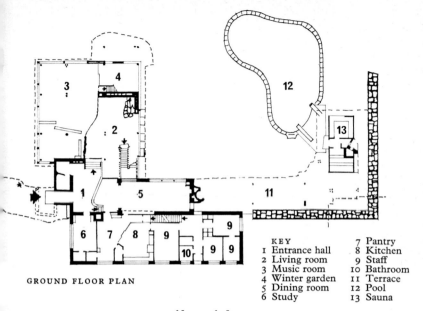

GROUND FLOOR PLAN

Alvar Aalto

VILLA MAIREA · NOORMARKKU · FINLAND · 1938

'Architectural chamber music which demands the strictest attention...'[1] Thus Professor Giedion has described this house, distinguished for its individual and sensitive handling of materials and for its rare combination of open planning and cosiness.

Aalto, more than any other architect, has demonstrated the significance of natural shapes and materials by the side of mechanical ones. He believes that architects have a moral obligation to answer the needs of society, and that design must remain adaptable to the different conditions of each site. Standardization therefore should be limited to doors, windows, mechanical equipment and structure.

Out of all this a human quality emerges, seen here in such details as the wicker wrapping shiny black columns, the bamboo poles on

[1] S. Giedion, *Space, Time and Architecture*, Harvard University Press, Cambridge, Mass., third edition, 1959.

VILLA MAIREA *Courtesy Museum of Finnish Architecture*

the staircase, and the granite slabs of the fireplace set against rough
plaster and painted brick.

Aalto also has a very personal way of handling space. Although
some of the windows are large and there are exterior spaces in the
form of balconies and porches, the principal effect is the result of
internal relationships. Professor Giedion[1] has pointed to the undu-
lating wall facing the entrance door and to the consequent diagonal
movements, first up the steps to the living room, then across to the
fireplace, and finally either up the staircase or into the large music
room. The double columns and the bamboo poles with their
narrow gaps, seem to emphasize this flow of space and at the same
time echo the rhythm of tree trunks in the forest around.

[1] *Ibid*

VILLA MAIREA *Courtesy Museum of Finnish Architecture*

VILLA MAIREA *Courtesy Mrs Gullichsen*

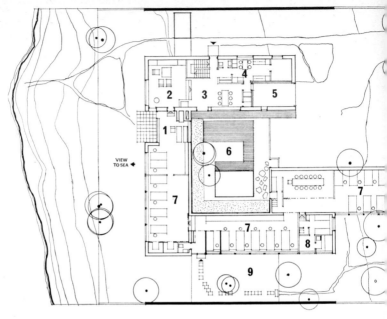

Kaija and Heikki Siren

SIREN HOUSE AND OFFICE · LAUTTASAARI
HELSINKI · FINLAND · COMPLETED 1960

This is the first example in this book to combine a family home with a full-scale office. It is also an example of the flexibility of modern design, as the office section had to be planned for expansion without affecting the unity of the conception as a whole. The first stage, the house and the office section at right-angles to the house, was built in 1951. The second and third stages, extending the office and providing it with a sauna bath and a conference room, were built in 1956 and 1960 respectively. The house, however, remains the dominant unit, with its high roof pitched like a chalet over the long dimension of the plan and accommodating upper floors of bedrooms.

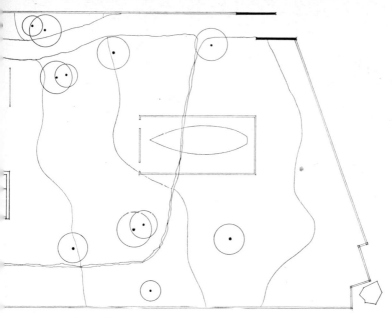

GROUND FLOOR PLAN

The plan is a combination of openness and enclosure. On one side it faces outwards to the sea, on another it looks on to sheltered courtyards. Both the office and the house can enjoy these contrasts. But while the entrance court to the office is an informal extension to the narrow and regimented internal space, the austere simplicity of the central court and swimming pool, with its geometric layout of wooden deck and shingle, forms a suitable complement to the more casual and intimate character of the house. The office turns its back on to this courtyard with blank walls, but the house opens up its broad gable end, as much as climate will allow, both on the ground and first floor, with windows, doors and balconies.

SIREN HOUSE AND OFFICE *Courtesy Kaija and Heikki Siren*

SIREN HOUSE AND OFFICE *Courtesy Kaija and Heikki Siren*

◁ SIREN HOUSE AND OFFICE
Aarne Pietinen

Friedhelm Thomas

Reinhard Gieselmann

HERZER HOUSE · KARLSRUHE−DURLACH · GERMANY 1960

The uncompromising look of this house, reminiscent of the concrete and white stucco houses of an earlier period, brings it closer to the Mediterranean south than to the Scandinavian north. Gieselmann indulges in the freedom of monolithic construction, cutting openings into a continuous white surface, around corners and in any shape or size, to form a strong abstract pattern like a painting by Ben Nicholson. The white top, which seems to float, is strongly articulated by cantilevers and by the contrasting rough texture of dark pebbles applied to the walls of the lower floor.

The site with its northern slope and access from the lower end determined an entrance on the road side and a living area on the high ground towards the back, to get a southerly outlook and be at garden level. The slope of the ground is also expressed in the penetration of the terrace, which is higher than the floor, into the living area in the form of a step or seat along the windows. The arrangement of levels is similar to Sörensen's house (page 86) except that here the bedrooms are above the entrance and on a higher level than the living area. From the entrance level, which also comprises a self-contained flat, short flights of stairs lead down to service quarters and up to the living area. This is openly planned with cooking and eating facilities and terraces, pergolas and a pool closely related to the interior.

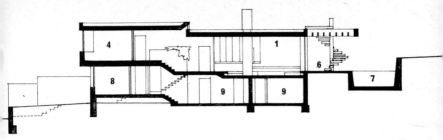

SECTION

KEY
1 Living room
2 Dining area
3 Kitchen
4 Bedrooms

5 Bathrooms
6 Terrace
7 Pool
8 Flat
9 Service and storage

UPPER FLOOR PLAN

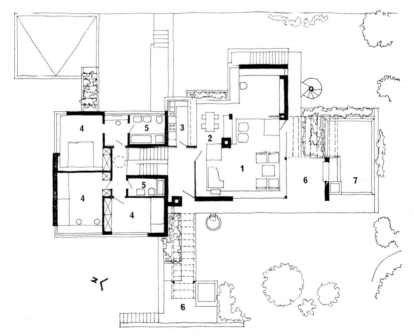

109

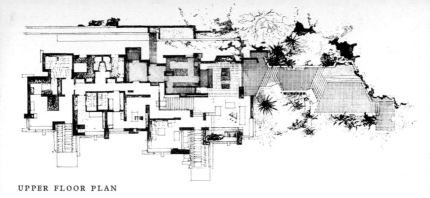

André Jacqmain

HOUSE AT RHODE-SAINT-GENÈSE · BRUSSELS
BELGIUM · 1960

The dream-like quality of this house was inspired by the client's collection of surrealist paintings. A labyrinth of concrete slabs, speckled with marble and gold enamel, seems to grow out of the earth like enormous stalagmites. The slabs with their irregular horizontal courses echoing the irregular vertical openings in the façade, seem to stand detached from the brick walls and windows behind. One such slab is in fact free-standing, like a sculpture on the lawn. Function has been subordinated to image for both receding brick and projecting concrete surfaces support floors and roofs.

The deep recessions in the façade create a feeling of ambiguity about indoors and out, especially on the ground floor where the openings are tall and narrow. The beautiful garden surrounded by a thick belt of azaleas and rhododendrons, seems to creep in everywhere and join up with the trees behind. But this too is an illusion confirmed by the enclosed character of the art gallery on the ground floor. Within this enclosure the labyrinthine character is maintained, enabling the visitor to choose many different paths and encouraging him to pause in front of a painting, or sit down and relax before continuing on his walk. The lighting is subtle and varied, described by Jacqmain as 'playing on the walls, reflecting itself and, sometimes, leaving in the shade an entire panel whose paintings adapt themselves in this subdued light'.

◁ HERZER HOUSE
Friedhelm Thomas

HOUSE AT RHODE-SAINT-GENÈSE   *H. Kessels*

HOUSE AT RHODE-SAINT-GENÈSE   *H. Kessels*

HOUSE AT RHODE-SAINT-GENÈSE   *H. Kessels*

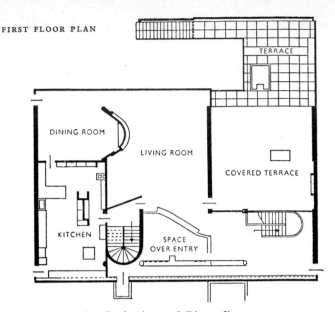

Le Corbusier and Pierre Jeanneret

HOUSE AT GARCHES · SEINE-ET-OISE · FRANCE 1927

Cubism attempted to show simultaneously the front, back and in-side of objects. But it was left to architecture to demonstrate the existence of time as a fourth dimension. Only in a building is it possible to appreciate the many-sided quality of space by moving from one point to another. Le Corbusier is as much a painter as an architect, and his early work in both arts is a faithful attempt to put these new concepts into practice.

This house, designed with blank end walls, suitable for its narrow suburban plot, is best appreciated in the light of the archi-tect's famous five points. First, floor and roof slabs are to be sup-ported entirely on free-standing columns, the medium being in-variably reinforced concrete. From this follows the second point, that all walls must be functionally independent of the skeleton structure. Here, the narrow strips of wall between windows are

literally hung from the edge of the projecting floor slabs, the columns rising within the building. Thirdly, *le plan libre*, meaning complete freedom to model the interior with curved or rectilinear partitions and staircases, and to break the inside open with terraces and ramps. This house has a particularly dramatic terrace on two levels which is open through two storeys, bringing the outside deep into the volume of the building. Fourthly, the façade can be free, but without rejecting order and discipline. In fact Le Corbusier often uses, as in this house, the golden section as a regulator. It means rather the freedom resulting from the absence of points of support in the façade and the possibility of using continuous bands of window. Lastly the roof garden is both an expression of liberation and a new surface to be explored and developed with screens and sunshades.

HOUSE AT GARCHES   *Courtesy Architectural Association*

HOUSE AT GARCHES   *Courtesy Architectural Association*

MAISON DE VERRE   *Michel Marty*

Chareau and Bijvoet

MAISON DE VERRE · 31 RUE ST GUILLAUME
PARIS · FRANCE · 1928–1931

This house of glass and steel displays a masterly grasp of technique, both in the main structure and in details such as sliding and pivoted doors, railway-carriage type windows, and pivoting cupboards and partitions dividing and screening bathrooms. It would be invidious to call it ahead of its time. In its conception it remains timeless and in its realisation, the elegant main staircase for example, at least the equal of the best today.

Pierre Chareau, who trained as an engineer and practised mainly as a designer of interiors, experimenting all his life with mobile furniture, built this house for Dr and Madame Dalsace, who still live there. An existing house had to be pulled down first, but as

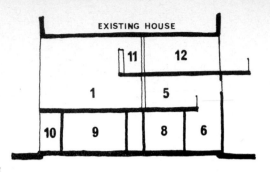

EXISTING HOUSE

SECTION

FIRST FLOOR PLAN

KEY
 1 Drawing room
 2 Dining room
 3 Kitchen
 4 Sitting room
 5 Study
 6 Well of ground floor
   waiting room
 7 Well of ground floor
   Doctor's office
 8 Receptionist's room
 9 Surgery
10 Entrance
11 Gallery
12 Bedrooms

an old lady living in the second and third floors refused to move, this upper part was supported on steel columns and the part underneath demolished. The new house provided consulting rooms on the ground floor and living accommodation on the first and second floors, an extra floor being fitted into the available height.

The quality which emerges is one of transparency and translucence. This is apparent in everything, from the outer walls to the staircases and bookshelves. The planning is open in the vertical direction. The Doctor's office, part of the waiting room and the drawing room are all double storey in height. Despite this openness, considerable privacy is maintained partly, no doubt, because of the numerous and independent means of communication between floors. Another reason may be that the translucent walls admit as much light as possible without letting the street or the neighbours infringe on the privacy of the interior. With the outside world unable to look in, the internal function of the building and its innate character as a town house is effectively stressed.

MAISON DE VERRE   *Michel Marty*

HOUSE AT ROTHRIST   *Albert Winkler*

Atelier 5 (Fritz, Gerber, Hesterberg, Hostettler, Morgenthaler, Pini and Thormann)

HOUSE AT ROTHRIST · NEAR OLTEN · SWITZERLAND
1958

'Stairs are a measure of civilization.' In this statement Auguste Perret demanded that architectural elements should express more than their function. The potentialities of steel and concrete have made the staircase a particularly suitable medium, and we have already noted its varied use and effect in the Maison de Verre (page 117). In this house the external staircase, leading up to the terrace with a comfortable rake, provides a sense of arrival that is in complete contrast to the almost subterranean entrance, whose vertical spiral staircase delivers the visitor into the middle of the house opposite a window with a dramatic view.

Although the house may owe something to Le Corbusier's (page 114) especially in the external staircase, terrace and balcony, in certain fundamental respects it is completely different. The construction consists of load-bearing walls of monolithic concrete into which various window openings have been cut. The walls act as an envelope, and the house is a series of largely enclosed but related spaces. The living room is two storeys high, with a gallery library, and has relatively small windows of different shapes framing con-

◁ MAISON DE VERRE
Michel Marty

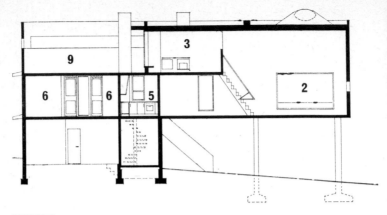

SECTION

FIRST FLOOR PLAN

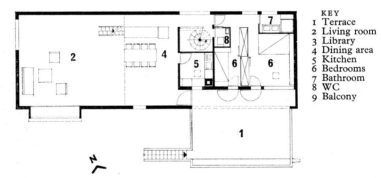

KEY
1 Terrace
2 Living room
3 Library
4 Dining area
5 Kitchen
6 Bedrooms
7 Bathroom
8 WC
9 Balcony

trasting views of orchards and mountains. A tilted dome in the roof provides diffused light for the owner's art collection. A sense of separation from the library is implied by the ladder-like stair-case which leads up to it, and by the high and solid balustrade at the edge of the gallery. Turning its back on to the living room, the library opens out on to a large balcony which is also mostly en-closed, except towards the sky, and forms a real outdoor room.

HOUSE AT ROTHRIST   *Albert Winkler*

HOUSE AT ROTHRIST   *Albert Winkler*

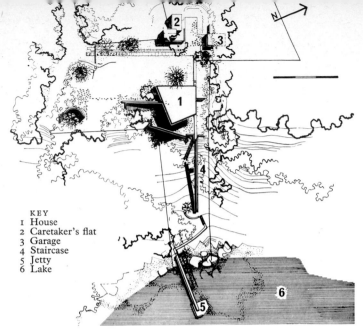

KEY
1 House
2 Caretaker's flat
3 Garage
4 Staircase
5 Jetty
6 Lake

SITE PLAN

Vittoriano Vigano

HOUSE AT VENTO BAY · LAKE GARDA · ITALY 1957

Probably the finest house built in Europe since the war, this also has the advantage of a secluded site dominating a magnificent view. Yet landscape of this grandeur must be considered a challenge to any architect. Vigano's achievement meets this challenge with rare self-assurance, both in his conception and his handling of concrete.

The house, which was built for an artist's summer holidays, sits on top of a hill at the point where the ground begins to fall away. It is tied to the jetty on the lake by a dramatic staircase, spanning a depression on the hillside and consisting of a concrete beam from which are cantilevered steel steps and balusters. The small house by itself might have remained a mere speck, but with the long pattern of the staircase it takes a significant form in the landscape.

124

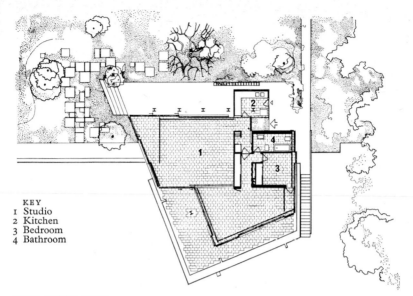

KEY
1 Studio
2 Kitchen
3 Bedroom
4 Bathroom

MAIN FLOOR PLAN

The scale throughout is entirely appropriate. The roughness of the staircase concrete, and the way in which the steel channels of the balustrade have simply been cut at a convenient height, would have seemed crude over a shorter length and in a setting of cultivated terraces. The house itself consists of two trapezoidal slabs—the floor and the roof—partly cantilevered and set with one angle tilted in the direction of the lake, so that the whole structure seems to be pushing forward into space. Between the slabs runs a wide concrete handrail, and with these three dominating lines the recessed window pattern remains subdued. From inside the studio the view is flattened into a panorama while, as a contrast, the study on the lower floor faces on to a planted courtyard.

HOUSE ON LAKE GARDA   *Courtesy Vittoriano Vigano*

HOUSE ON LAKE GARDA   *Allegri*

HOUSE ON LAKE GARDA   *Courtesy Vittoriano Vigano*

Courtesy Pietro Lingeri

Pietro Lingeri

VILLA LEONI · LAKE COMO · ITALY · 1940

Lingeri belongs to the founders of modern Italian architecture. He
had known the short and powerful Futurist movement and had once
worked for its chief advocate, Sant'Elia. When Futurism petered
out with Sant'Elia's death and the disillusionment of the post-war
years, a group of young architects centred on Milan founded the
Rationalist movement, resisting throughout the long fascist years
the favoured rhetorical style. The Rationalists, like the Futurists,
sought to express the new concepts of space with the new materials,
but unlike the Futurists, did not reject trabeated forms of construction on the grounds that they lacked the necessary dynamic
qualities.

Lingeri's house overlooking Lake Como can best be appreciated

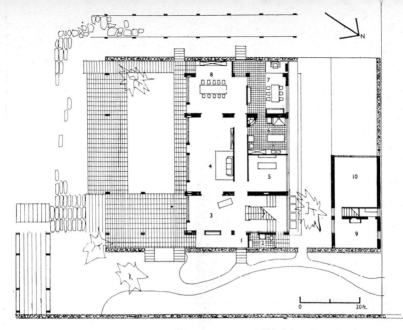

GROUND FLOOR PLAN   KEY

1 Entrance	6 Kitchen	
2 Cloakroom	7 Breakfast room	
3 Hall	8 Dining room	
4 Sitting room	9 Servants' living room	
5 Study	10 Garage	

through an examination of its structure. The load-bearing cross-walls, leaving large openings on two sides, are eminently suitable for a hilly site with a view. All the living rooms and bedrooms face the lake. The construction is boldly expressed by projecting the cross-walls beyond the window line and these projections carry balconies both at bedroom level and on the solarium above. Their importance becomes evident from the low angle at which the front must always be seen, forcing one to look up and underneath. As a complete contrast to this sharp perspective, the sequence of ground floor rooms, with their close relation to the terrace, forms a vast and calm square platform defined by a single line of posts and beams.

VILLA LEONI

VILLA LEONI

Courtesy Pietro Lingeri

Courtesy Pietro Lingeri

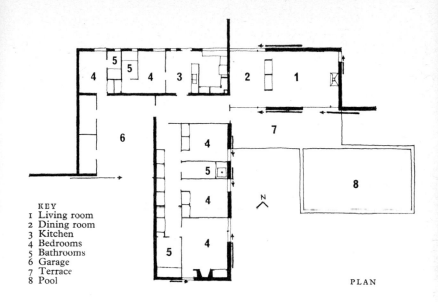

KEY
1 Living room
2 Dining room
3 Kitchen
4 Bedrooms
5 Bathrooms
6 Garage
7 Terrace
8 Pool

PLAN

Coderch and Valls

HOUSE AT SITGES · BARCELONA · SPAIN · 1957

In their effort to arrive at functional solutions architects often look towards vernacular traditions in building, as an example of form which has evolved slowly from local conditions and use. This house undoubtedly belongs to a Mediterranean tradition of simple white cubes thrown into relief by the sun. Yet the architects have avoided any suggestion of folk art in their rational treatment of the exterior and in the unaffected simplicity of the fittings and furniture, which they designed themselves. In the words of the Japanese architect Kenzo Tange, 'tradition must be like a catalyst that disappears once its task is done'. The use of light and shade in the deep overhang of the roof, in the delicate texture of the shutters and in the angle formed by two plain walls coming together, reflects the essence rather than the manner of a style.

131

HOUSE AT SITGES   *F. Catala Roca*

The articulated plan, which provides accommodation for a
family of four, guests and servants, is highly functional, and the
construction is of local materials—bricks and tiles—and reinforced
concrete, structural timber not being easily available. The roof
over the service and bedroom blocks is not expressed, and these
two units are largely enclosed, with only a few openings on one of
their sides. The living room block, on the other hand, opens up to
the north with a projecting wall and to the south with an overhanging roof, a terrace and a pool.

HOUSE AT SITGES   *F. Catala Roca*
HOUSE AT SITGES   *F. Catala Roca*

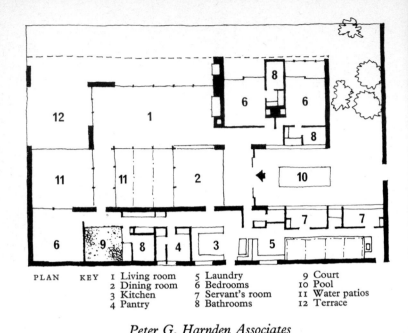

PLAN	KEY	1 Living room	5 Laundry	9 Court
		2 Dining room	6 Bedrooms	10 Pool
		3 Kitchen	7 Servant's room	11 Water patios
		4 Pantry	8 Bathrooms	12 Terrace

Peter G. Harnden Associates

HOUSE NEAR ALHAURIN DE LA TORRE · MALAGA SPAIN · 1960

Although neither client nor architect was Spanish, this house, too, is traditional, both in its use of local materials and in its Andalusian plan of two parallel fingers with courtyards in between. It has distant views of the bay of Malaga and the Sierra Nevada and its siting, following Frank Lloyd Wright's principle, is *around* the brow of a hill, not *on top*. Winter winds, the heat in summer and the isolated nature of the site, determined an inward-looking plan. Within the rectangle, mainly enclosed on three sides by forbidding stone walls, there are several courtyards and terraces which let the light and air into the middle of the building, providing cross-ventilation and, in the sequence of water patios, a welcome contrast to the arid surroundings.

HOUSE NEAR MALAGA   *Casali*

The client's brief asked, among other things, for a house of restrained character and suitable for highly civilized living. There were to be few rooms, a feeling of great space and no ostentation whatever. Except for the bedrooms and service area, the house is an elaborate and continuous open space, punctuated by light and dark areas. Standing in the cool entrance hall, we look through the dining area into an open court, through a glazed corridor and into another court shut off by a stone wall. Diagonally towards the right the living room leads on to an L-shaped terrace of contrasting character, one part being completely open and the other partly protected by three short sections of stone wall acting both as screens and as foils to the landscape.

135

HOUSE NEAR MALAGA   *Casali*

HOUSE NEAR MALAGA   *Casali*

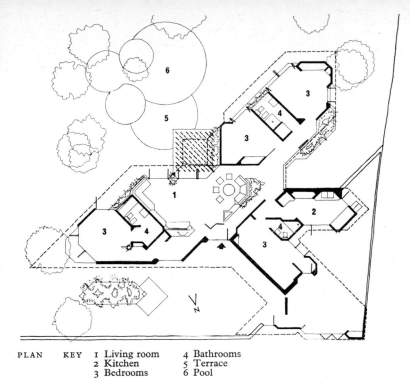

PLAN KEY
1 Living room   4 Bathrooms
2 Kitchen   5 Terrace
3 Bedrooms   6 Pool

Franco d'Ayala Valva

HOUSE NEAR CUERNAVACA · MEXICO · 1959

Although the modern movement did not really come to the Latin American countries until a few years before the Second World War, it has since made a major contribution there in the development of reinforced concrete techniques, especially curved forms. The lack of steel manufacturers and shortage of structural timber has concentrated all efforts on this method of construction, and it is largely thanks to Brazil, for instance, that the building raised on stilts has been established in the public image.

In Mexico more than in Brazil the influence of Colonial and

HOUSE NEAR CUERNAVACA *Courtesy Franco d'Ayala Valva*

Indian traditions, especially on smaller buildings, has provided a salutary opposition to the international style based on a technology that is supposed to have no frontiers. D'Ayala himself says of the glass-fronted living rooms, 'is not the need of protecting the interior from the glaring Mexican sun and light by heavy curtains, the proof of a sacrifice and of a refusal to face an integrally organized space?' Spanish colonial buildings were usually inward-looking and defensive in character, and this house, turning its back on to a village square, follows this tradition. On the other side it opens out on to a tropical garden, but this is entirely surrounded by a wall built of local volcanic stone. The enclosed and protected nature of the house is stressed by the predominance of the tiled roof, consisting of several overlapping triangular prisms which seem to float over the deeply recessed walls and windows. This is continued internally through the expression of the various roof slopes inside the rooms.

HOUSE NEAR CUERNAVACA   *Courtesy Franco d'Ayala Valva*

HOUSE NEAR CUERNAVACA   *Courtesy Franco d'Ayala Valva*

Luis Barragan

BARRAGAN HOUSE · TUCUBAYA · MEXICO DF
1948

Luis Barragan was not trained as an architect, but he shows a far
greater feeling for space and form than most members of the pro-
fession. His own office, studio and house combined, demonstrates
these qualities in the play of light and shade on the balcony roof,
in the library staircase utterly simplified without even a handrail,
and in the street façade which also fits in perfectly with its neighbours. Barragan, much more than d'Ayala, is a traditionalist who
uses walls as envelopes to mould interior spaces and who, in his
handling of natural materials and indigenous textiles, conceives
decoration as an integral part of a building. The large windows in
the library and studio, for instance, have fixed glazing, the ways
out into the garden being slightly apart and quite narrow. They
are there for the view they give, 'for the tropical climate of the
place, its natural "dirtiness",' to quote d'Ayala again, 'marks a very
sharp division between interior and exterior and nature becomes
only a show to be seen and not lived with in close relationship'.
Here the show is a beautiful garden design by Barragan himself, a
talent which he was to display the following year on a far grander
scale in his layout for the gardens of Pedregal.

◁ HOUSE NEAR CUERNAVACA
Courtesy Franco d'Ayala Valva

ELEVATION TO STREET

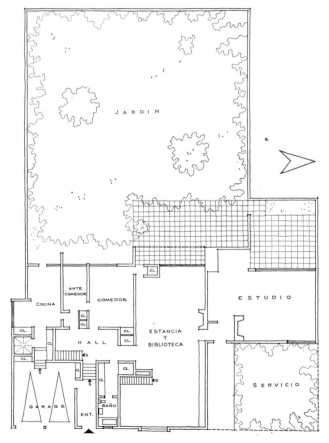

JARDIN

ANTE
COMEDOR

COMEDOR

COCINA

CL.

CL.
CL.

CL.

CL.

CL.

ESTUDIO

CL.

ESTANCIA
Y
BIBLIOTECA

CL.

CL.

HALL

CL.

CL.

S

S

S

GARAGE

BAÑO

ENT.

SERVICIO

GROUND FLOOR PLAN

BARRAGAN HOUSE
Armando Salas Portugal

BARRAGAN HOUSE   *Armando Salas Portugal*

BARRAGAN HOUSE   *Armando Salas Portugal*

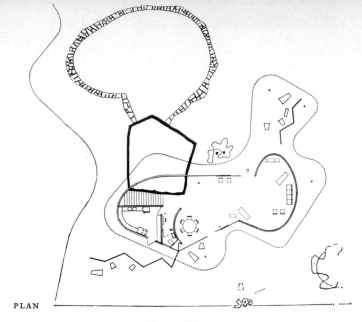

PLAN

Oscar Niemeyer

NIEMEYER HOUSE · GAVEA · RIO DE JANEIRO
BRAZIL · 1953–1954

Twice in the history of Brazilian architecture has the influence of France been of fundamental importance. Once in 1816 when French sculptors, painters and architects were invited by the government to direct and teach, establishing a style which lasted over a hundred years; and a second time in 1929 when Le Corbusier came over from Paris to lecture. He came again in 1935 to act as consultant for the new Ministry of Education in Rio, for which Lucio Costa had been appointed architect with Niemeyer as one of the associates. Today two influences exist side by side. On the one hand, the initial impetus given by Le Corbusier to a talented and active group of native architects has developed into a plastic style which has almost become part of tradition; on the other, architecture in the United States, especially that of Mies van der Rohe and his fol-

NIEMEYER HOUSE   *Nicolau Drei*

lowers, has made its mark on the younger generation of Brazilian
architects.

Niemeyer's house, built for himself, is a unique lyrical statement
in concrete. Gropius has called him 'bird of paradise', and indeed
neither house nor landscape quite belong to this world. It becomes
part of the natural setting, not by merging like Harnden's granite
walls (page 134), but through its organic form that looks like a great
outcrop of rock, part of which has been left untouched, the rest
having been scooped out, levelled and polished. To obtain the freedom of design which he required, Niemeyer has relegated the bedrooms to a lower floor. Under the roof slab, screens and glass
enclose the living area, but these, functionally laid out as they are,
bear little relation to the wild shape of the roof.

NIEMEYER HOUSE

NIEMEYER HOUSE *R. Maia & Franceschi*

BRATKE HOUSE

Osvaldo Arthur Bratke

BRATKE HOUSE · SAO PAULO · BRAZIL · 1953

The geometric discipline of this house and the clear expression of its structure may reflect the influence of Mies van der Rohe, but the use of materials and the effect of the concrete sun-screens—a typically Brazilian feature—are entirely individual.

The house is planned on a grid but, within the rectangle formed by the structure and on a continuous floor slab raised above the ground even at the upper level, walls and windows are set back on different planes, to give protection against the sun and to form a planted pool and a balcony. In particular should be noted the sun screen to the library, which stands forward on the line of the structure in contrast to the window and screen to the living room, which are set back overlooking the pool. On the east side the living room opens out on to a terrace defined by a low wall, with a fine view over Sao Paulo.

149

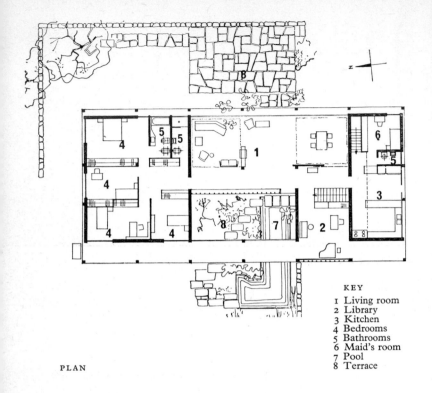

KEY
1 Living room
2 Library
3 Kitchen
4 Bedrooms
5 Bathrooms
6 Maid's room
7 Pool
8 Terrace

PLAN

In contrast to Niemeyer's house (page 146) there is no suggestion
whatever of a form emerging out of the landscape. On the contrary,
this house is firmly set on top of its site, a sophisticated man-made
object. Only the slope of the ground has been used in a similar way,
by providing an entrance on a lower floor.

BRATKE HOUSE
BRATKE HOUSE

Ernesto Mandowsky
F. Albuquerque

MARTINS HOUSE

Amancio d'Alpoim Guedes
MARTINS HOUSE · LOURENÇO MARQUES
MOZAMBIQUE · 1953

'. . . The truth is that Art Nouveau aborted because there was no one with the imagination needed to take it through.'[1] Guedes re-asserts an age-old tradition of plastic forms and the artist's duty to create memorable symbols like the ancient pyramids and temples. Descending from Iberian Baroque and the Art Nouveau of Gaudi, his work is characteristic of those extravagant tendencies to be found in the southern extremities of Latin Europe. It seems entirely appropriate transplanted to a Portuguese colony with a hot damp climate and a tropical vegetation. This house rises out of a jungle of plants and trees like a colossal mushroom. Nature has been

[1] *Architectural Review*, London, April, 1961

Courtesy A. d'Alpoim Guedes

allowed to conceal most of the ground floor, so that the roofs and chimneys dominate.

The remarkable work of Guedes must be seen against the local background. Building methods are primitive and labour cheap, the standard material being concrete. But the technique of shuttering is so poor that all buildings have to be plastered. Guedes has his group of workmen who have become skilled with reinforced concrete, and he himself works on the site much of the time. One workman has even been trained to carry out his concrete sculptures and another his murals of coloured pebbles, these works of art being sold to any willing client at cost price.

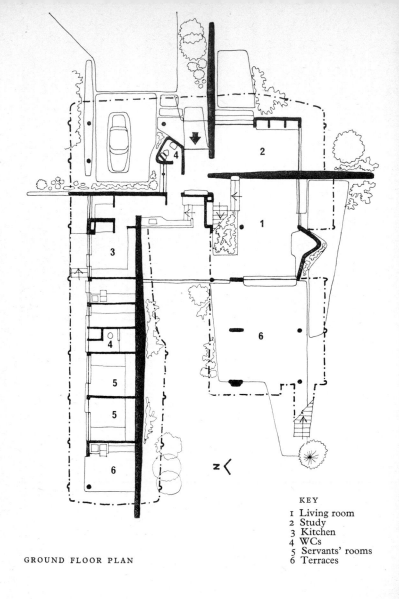

z ‹

KEY

1 Living room
2 Study
3 Kitchen
4 WCs
5 Servants' rooms
6 Terraces

GROUND FLOOR PLAN

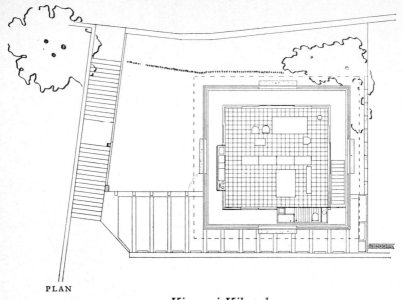

PLAN

Kiyonori Kikutake
THE SKY HOUSE · OTOWA · TOKYO · JAPAN
1958–1959

Kikutake is one of the leaders of the new Metabolism Group, started in 1960, which conceives architecture as dynamic open form, infinitely adaptable to the changes of the future. His own imaginative idea for sky and water cities may one day become reality in a country that is acutely short of building land. The Sky house, on the other hand, is already built and proof of the validity of these ideas.

It is a large square space, raised high above the rooftops of the surrounding wooden buildings and supported on four wide concrete piers. The danger of earthquakes partly determined the form of the structure, namely few points of support and a light paraboloid roof. The interior is a single room, subdivided by a low wall of cupboards and unencumbered by the kitchen and bathroom, which

SKY HOUSE   Y. *Futagawa*

take up some of the surrounding balcony. Thus the central space is
permanent, fulfilling spiritual needs, while the compact units—
bathroom, kitchen and children's room (which is designed to be
suspended under the floor when required)—are changeable when
their efficiency has been superseded or their use has passed.

The Sky house has also been called the 'House of Light'. To
get the more subtle evening effects of sunlight it was made to face
south-west. The living area is high and open on all sides, but light
can be controlled with any number of variations, by the shutters
which slide along the edge of the balcony and by the paper screens
which slide across the windows. At night concealed fluorescent
lights illuminate the floor surface all round, while movable paper
lanterns suggest the individual activities of a family house.

SKY HOUSE   *Y. Futagawa*

SKY HOUSE   *Y. Futagawa*

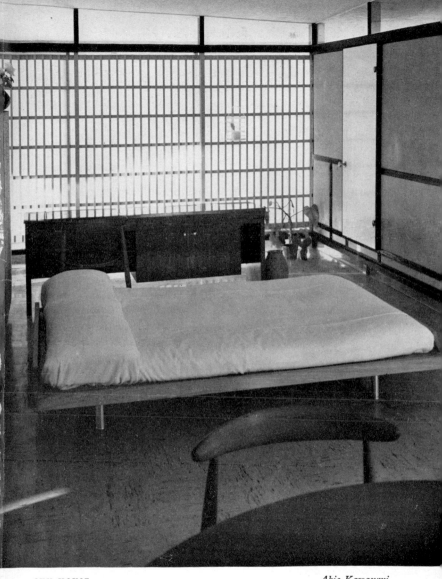

SKY HOUSE   *Akio Kawasumi*

BIBLIOGRAPHICAL NOTE

The most complete bibliography of general and specific subjects covering the whole period of modern architecture is to be found in *Architecture: Nineteenth and Twentieth Centuries* by Henry-Russell Hitchcock, in the 'Pelican History of Art' series, Penguin Books (1958). This should be supplemented for the United States by the bibliography in Ian McCallum's book, *Architecture U.S.A.*, Architectural Press, London, 1959. In addition to *The Master Builders* (Frank Lloyd Wright, Mies van der Rohe and Le Corbusier), by Peter Blake, which has already been mentioned, Prentice-Hall International have been publishing three valuable series: the first, 'Masters of World Architecture', includes monographs on Sullivan, Wright, Neutra, Mies, Gropius, Mendelsohn, Aalto, Le Corbusier, Niemeyer, Gaudi and Nervi; the second, 'Makers of Contemporary Architecture', monographs on Kahn, Fuller, Johnson, Saarinen and Tange; and the third, 'Great Ages of World Architecture', an interesting essay entitled 'Modern Architecture' by Vincent Scully, Jr, which includes a useful bibliographical note. There is also now a monograph, *The Work of G. Rietveld, Architect*, by Theodore M. Brown, A. W. Bruna & Zoon, Utrecht, 1958.

Finally the most valuable sources are the professional periodicals and, for contemporary houses, especially *Architectural Design* in England, *Architecture d'Aujourd'hui* in France, *Domus* and *Casabella* in Italy, and *Architectural Record*, *Architectural Forum* and *Arts and Architecture* in the United States.